Contents

If She Can Change So Can You!

I'll never forget my Mother-In-Law, Marian's words 15 years ago during another heated argument about holidays or gifts or whatever, but certainly some relatively meaningless battle. She said "I'm too old to change" (she was all of 50 or so at the time). When she uttered those words, the argument at hand was futile and my perceptions and frustrations were altered not just for the moment, but for the long-term.

But here we are in 2011 and I've got to say – my relationship with my Mother-in-Law is better than it ever was. Much better. She is a terrific grandparent to our teenage children and a damn good mother-in-law as well. And while she may not admit it, she has changed... significantly. Changed in ways that has strengthened our family dynamics and changed in subtle ways that I can't quite put my finger on. I like being around her, I like talking to her, I no longer have trepidation or fear in when the next argument will be. And she probably would say the same thing about her daughter Nancy (and my wonderful wife) and I. The change has been evident in us in all of us collaboratively to allow for a richer relationship for everyone's benefit.

I share my Mother-In-Law example so you too can be self-reflective. Ask yourself, "How can I enhance my business & personal brand to make myself more likable, more promotable, more aware, more hirable, more exceptional, more intellectual, more dependable and a zillion other traits that allow you to recognize that your ability to enhance your business performance and your Companies performance or perhaps, land your next job is not about those around you.

This is about YOU.

This Bleeping Book

I've been saying bad words a bit too often the last couple of months. You see, 10 years ago (maybe more), my wife Nancy suggested I write a book, a collection of my quarterly business recommendations remitted to clients and prospective clients called *TouchPoints*. *TouchPoints* recipients have consistently praised the content as quite valuable to overcome their business challenges.

Despite Nancy's insistence, I resisted…, too many other priorities. And then three years ago, I developed my new business model, 10 Minutes to Change™ and so many business colleagues have urged… "What a Great Name. What a Brilliant Concept.! You Have to Write a Book!"

I've learned, you must listen to the crowd and the book has become a priority. I wrote and organized, wrote and organized, but somewhere along the way lost energy and put the book down for another period of hibernation, 9 months or so ago.

I don't quite remember what has re-kindled my motivation the last six months of focused effort. Perhaps a direct response to another colleagues urging, maybe that internal fire ignited deep in the unconscious mind of Eric Frankel. But I am proud to say, despite the years of procrastination, despite the pain and effort required to put this book in a finished, high quality format, despite the incessant complaining to Nancy that I have to write this bleeping book, that in my humble opinion, this bleeping book is pretty damn good.

I hope you agree.

Utilize This Book to
Optimize Your Personal Brand

Each of the chapters herein are comprised of random thoughts and wisdom I've gathered and observed over the last 16 years of running a diversified management consulting company. These *TouchPoints* are designed to be read in quick intervals, 10 minutes here, 20 minutes there, whatever your time permits.

As you flip through the pages, I caution you to not just focus on the ideas relevant to you and your organization- focus on the concepts "outside your box" to think twice about others' experience and perspectives.

Some of the ideas here will pique your interest. Note them with a pen for future reference. For these, spend 10 minutes of your time reflecting on "Why".

Some of the ideas here will not be relevant. Move on.

Some of the ideas will be in the middle. Use your own judgment of what to do.

Read this book to maximize yourself as a well-rounded business person, to better relate to your peers and to optimize your unique and ever expanding Personal Brand. Strive to be that business professionals others' view as multi-faceted, "well-rounded", a great listener and sounding board. Make sure that diversified is an adjective which describes you, now and in the future.

The ideas which pique your interest will allow you to look inward to impact your business confidence, your organizational skills, and your desire to "act of your box", making you more fulfilled, interesting and impacting for the benefit of those whom you touch.

Here's to Good Changes!

Utilize This Book to Optimize Your Personal Brand

1

Interpersonal Skills Empower YOU!

The concept of EQ (emotional quotient) vs. IQ (intelligence quotient) has achieved prominence the last 20 years. In business we simply say those who "get it" vs. those "who don't". An employees' ability to positively impact others dictates their success, individually and organizationally.

§ **Control E-Mail** - Email has tremendous benefits including ease of use, low cost, and transfer of files. Unfortunately, the proliferation of this tool (not to mention texting etc.) is creating serious time, production and perhaps most important, people inefficiencies. E-mail is inferior to direct communication (i.e. telephone, in-person), drains key management time in the sorting and reading process, and invites employee abuse and misinterpretation.

§ **Are You Multi-Faceted Or A Multi-Faceter?** - Attractive is multi-faceted, the professional who excels with multiple priorities and possesses strong confidence, presence and business knowhow. Annoying is the multi-faceter, the individual juggling multiple tasks at a moment in time (smart-phone, telephone, computer) when 100% attention should be on the conversation at hand.

§ Ask Questions To Enhance Knowledge & Power -
As I often tell my children, the only bad question is the one you don't ask. In business and in life, ask for what you want and you will often receive.

§ Don't Wait For Thank You – Leaders must be confident
in their own skills and actions, and recognize that employees are extremely unlikely to say "thank you" for anything. They will show gratitude through their work effort… not their words. In the same vein, executive managers must improve their level of approachability. Minimize body language that reflects irritation or lack of patience. Employees should always feel comfortable approaching their supervisors, one and two levels higher.

§ Deliver Criticism Properly – Always deliver negative
communication behind closed doors in combination with constructive feedback, where practical. When very frustrated with a situation, step back before taking actions you will regret to allow resolution in a proactive, rather than reactive manner.

§ Keep In Mind The Value Of Snail Mail - The least
crowded way to garner decision maker attention is US mail. For client/vendor initiatives and follow up to interviews, don't underestimate the value of name recognition with a well-written letter or thank you (ideally handwritten if legible).

§ Deliver Great Service, Receive Great Dividends -
Recently, my wife Nancy did something which makes a world of sense; she made sure excellent service was recognized. While enjoying a meal w/extended family, we were impressed by our waitress who greatly enhanced our dining experience. In addition to a solid tip, Nancy did one better by informing the restaurant owner this woman had earned our utmost respect.

Ideally, the waitress and the restaurant will now earn more and other patrons will enjoy a dining experience similar to our own. While we are often frustrated by bad service (and let them know about it), let's make sure we praise superior interactions as well. Let's pay it forward.

§ This Is Why I Use Facebook! -
Over the last year, three former "acquaintances", all fellow UConn alumni have sought me out. In two instances, the women were friends and I've really enjoyed "catching up" regarding our respective family and business successes.

The other situation was more nebulous. I didn't recognize the name or the picture associated with the invite. But then she said and I quote, " I remember crying to you that I was going to fail cost accounting with James -- right was that his name -- and I ended up really "getting it" after you explained it to me! I think I have a picture of you from graduation -- I'll have to post it if I can find it!" Jean found the picture and now I remember! Thanks Jean for making my day and helping me to remember my mentoring skills 25 years ago went a long way towards helping others. And thank you, Facebook!

2

Talent Retention and Ascension

The Human Resource function is amplifying their impact in many companies from the conference room to the boardroom. Organizations are realizing and slowly embracing the immense, but often intangible benefits of talent acquisition, motivation, engagement and collaboration.

§ **Consistently "Sell" Your Company** - From beginning to end of the interview process, prospective employees should be highly intrigued about your organization. The ability to attract top quality employees is dictated by their instincts in combination with the perception you provide of your "Company atmosphere".

§ **Hire Strangers, not Friends** - Companies often hire friends, friends of friends, relatives, and relatives of friends in staffing for open positions. Hiring in this manner has occasional merit, but there is no better way to staff a Company than hiring in the open job market with quality internal managers to assess and train. Nepotism spawns "cliques", taking of sides, negativity and counterproductive rumors.

§ **Is a B.S. Always Cost Effective?** - Expand your recruiting initiatives to include professionals without college degrees. These candidates often require less compensation and over time, have greater company loyalty.

§ **Make Sure the Candidate is Right** – Interview managerial candidates in a job search a minimum of two, perhaps even three times to ensure consistency of communication and positive "vibes" in all discussions.

§ **The Obvious Value of In-Person Evaluation** - Always meet managerial talent face to face before hiring. Phone or video communications are fine interim communications, but should not be the basis for an affirmative decision.

§ **Don't Settle When It Comes to Recruiting** - In any business climate, recruiting highly competent, realistically priced professionals is a core challenge. Don't ever rush into making a hiring decision that just doesn't feel right in your gut. For this reason alone, temp employment will continue to grow as a viable and winning strategy for Companies.

§ **"Sell" to your Industry Specific Talent** - Focused efforts to cultivate relationships with and impress industry specific talent will drive your recruiting initiatives- short-term, mid-term and long-term. Develop a database of quality candidates with all contact information; utilize a combination of email, phone and mailing tactics to keep your brand in front of them (and their network).

§ Limit Reliance on Personality Profiles - Utilizing tests to ensure candidate adequacy is overrated. In the case of an excellent candidate, their fit and upside will be obvious. Only where you are "on the fence" might there be true value added from the testing process.

§ Prove That You Can! - If hunting & cold calling is part of the job requirement, require as part of the interview process 5 cold calls to prospective clients. This will weed out people who say they can sell, but lack recognition of the true challenges in prospecting and door opening.

§ The ABC's of Interviewing Etiquette - In job search, candidates are forced fed the "dos and don'ts" – do dress for success, don't ask about benefits, blah, blah, blah. Employers must also evaluate their own actions, as well, to attract from the shrinking pool of top echelon talent. Go after your gotta have candidates like a hot sales opportunity, don't presume your managers know how to interview or sell, and recognize candidates are "turned off" by extended waiting times and multi-tasking interviewers (i.e. all form of interruptions).

§ Ten Core Interview Questions to Assess Candidates:

1. Provide a 3 minute overview of your career? (Be concerned if they respond with a 30 second or 15 minute answer).
2. What was your best job and why? Your worst job?
3. Why did you decide to go into HR/sales/operations/accounting etc.?
4. What makes you an effective business person?
5. Why does our Company interest you?

6. What makes you effective in dealing with people (subordinates, peers, executives or external relationships)?
7. Where do you expect to be in 5 years?
8. What differentiates you from others seeking this position?
9. How do you organize your ideas, tasks and priorities?
10. Why do you consider yourself to be a team player? A good manager (if relevant)?

§ **Embrace the "R" in Human "R"esources** – While employee relations, compensation, benefits and strategy are important, the generalist HR Leader must embrace and enjoy recruiting. Many do not. Recruiting is a huge determinant in driving talent management, leadership development, organizational structure and growth.

§ **Look "Outward" for New Talent** - Requiring industry specific experience in non-technical job functions (i.e. sales, admin, accounting, HR) can be expensive and counterproductive. After the "honeymoon period" (three-six months), a quality employee without industry experience will far outshine an average employee with industry experience.

§ **Relieve the First Day Jitters** - There should be a clearly defined "first day" for new employees including a sit-down/overview with relevant department managers, and an acclimation period that allows them to feel comfortable and understand business basics. Their department manager should plan lunch (ideally on Day 1, but the first week is OK) and include peers. The concept of "On-Boarding" is highly relevant to ensure the learning and engagement curves are set in motion immediately.

§ Hire Slow, Fire Fast - Go with your gut not only for hiring purposes, but also for existing employees not performing up to par. Cut ties with recently hired employees within 90 days if behavior, performance or intangibles are in question and they do not respond to immediate communications to "step it up".

§ Improve Housing of Creative Ideas - Too often, creative ideas are "here today, gone tomorrow" due to focus on the daily priorities and a lack of proper "storage". Get employees away from paper to-do lists and encourage use of Microsoft Outlook tasks (or a 2nd calendar); more permanent, efficient and you don't have to re-create thoughts continuously.

§ Provide On the Job, Not Off the Job Training - Reading business books and attending training classes will not transform an employee from good to great. Most employees have limitations and hit an apex at some point in their career. Ensure your key managers are focused on a collaborative environment predicated on knowledge sharing and mutual respect to keep things interesting and keep all employees, apex or not, truly engaged.

§ Can You Sell or Can You Manage?-Well compensated employees (say $100K or above) and "up and comers" in an organization must possess one of two traits; they impact revenues or they impact fellow employees. Take a look at key employees in your organization to determine whether they possess either (or both) to effectively evaluate potential and compensation.

§ **Make a Goal of Setting Goals** - Heighten departmental accountability by requiring core simple, measurable goals on a quarterly basis for both recurring and nonrecurring tasks. Goal setting programs stimulate creativity and proactive thinking, clarify departmental focus, and better define (and monitor) employee performance.

§ **Solving the Jigsaw** - Think of organizational structure like a puzzle, usually a complex one. Solving the puzzle requires hands-on knowledge of employee competencies, collaborative thinking and strong, efficient decision making.

§ **Develop the Middle Management Team** - Sustained business growth hinges upon developing quality middle management talent. Executive management creates the vision and focus, middle management carries the torch. Managers must deliver on employee development, client satisfaction, and daily task execution. Executive management must harness the middle management team to be cohesive, skilled, accountable and responsive.

§ **It's Not Just "About the Money"** - High satisfaction and low turnover is prominent where managers trust employees (and in turn, employee's trust managers), flexibility is provided (i.e. reasonable personal time and phone calls), performance expectations are understood, tokens of appreciation (lunch, $25 Amex certificates) are provided, and of course, constructive and positive communication occurs genuinely, consistently and effectively.

§ Tread Softly When Terminating Employees - There are four "safe" ways to terminate an employee- poor performance within 90 days of start date, elimination of the actual job position, layoff (a healthy step in many Companies- but make sure you get it right) or termination for cause- supported by ongoing documentation. Because employee lawsuits (or even the threat of one) are incredibly debilitating, ensure you have a solid employment attorney to consult with before any and all personnel reductions.

§ Are They Talking the Same Language? - Be wary of key functional managers who don't communicate effectively regarding their areas of accountability. Ask them to simplify their goals, data, benefits and results to allow for sounder decision making, improved camaraderie with peers and in turn, increased revenues, margins and profits.

§ Understanding and Applying 'The Pareto Principle' - Vilfredo Pareto was a prominent early 20th century sociologist. His theories have significant business application. The Pareto Principle states that companies typically derive 80% of revenues from 20% of customers- appropriate care, focus and service should be provided to these "A" Customers. Utilizing this concept will instill richer organizational success to:

- **Motivate Employees** - One out of every five employees is likely to be a star. Identify the high-potentials and focus on developing their skills to benefit the employees around them. The other four employees may have critical job functions, but keep performance expectations realistic.

- **Manage Priorities** - Defining key tasks is a common challenge. Typically, only 20% of the items require immediate action, while others can be delegated or put on next day or week status. Frequent reprioritization is essential.

- **Streamline the Structure** - Limit direct reports for any one manager to 5. Create supervisors/line manager positions when this number is exceeded to ensure effective focus on planning, creating and implementing.

- **Meet Your Long-Term Goals** - Of your peers, only one out of five has achieved success comparable to yours. Defining and attaining the "next level" will require supreme confidence (in yourself and your people), vision and fortitude. Only 20% of your current peers will get there.

3

The Complex Rungs Of Managerial Success

Not everyone given a special title has the innate ability, confidence and will to succeed. Are you one of them?

§ **You Can't Be a Manager Without Managing** - Managers and executive managers must spend a minimum of 25% of their time developing talent, recognizing a top priority is responding to subordinate needs. This leaves the skills of many with Manager/Director/VP titles exposed. Lack of managerial oversight is a sure-fire reason for dissatisfaction, inefficiency and inequitable workloads.

§ **Delegate, Delegate and then Delegate** – Every manager must delegate (or plan the path towards such) as much of their day to day responsibilities as feasible. Take this newfound time to develop talent, increase direct communication with internal and external colleagues, and fine-tune/drive your tactical and strategic goals.

§ **Process Documentation Doesn't Always Make Sense** – You need quality personnel, consistency of action and effective infrastructure before devising flowcharts, internal controls and process which can truly be adhered to.

§ Develop Relationships in a Relaxed Setting -
Encourage managers to have breakfast or lunch with their peers and direct reports. This more relaxed environment builds rapport, teamwork, and removes obstacles that may exist behind organizational walls.

§ Don't Let Personnel Issues Drag You Down – One
of the most disruptive daily business challenges is a lack of cohesion amongst employees. These complexities are stressful, chaotic and often petty. Hoping interpersonal friction will "go away" only exacerbates the problems and negatively impacts Company performance. Resolution requires facilitated communication, two way conversations, implementation of performance management tools and a savvy HR function.

§ Problems = Solutions - Train every employee to bring
problems to light immediately, so that the "cause" may be examined, and recurrences are prevented.

§ Are You 98.6? - Take a quick business temperature by
simply asking; Are my employees happy and motivated? Am I?

§ Don't Bother with Goals Without a True Commitment - Goal performance systems are wasted
effort if not supported by timely and consistent follow through.

§ The Importance of Timely Employee Reviews - An employee remembers the late annual review long after the % salary increase has been forgotten. Make timely reviews a recurring goal and essential priority for all managerial personnel.

§ Positive Feedback Motivates – Small talk - i.e. "how was your weekend", pats on the back, even for something that was expected, delivers the message "we care". Occasional informal socials and functional/company interactions (i.e. bagel, pizza days) with employee groups all derive positive goodwill.

§ Maximize Meeting Effectiveness - Meetings are most effective when regularly scheduled, stick to a succinct time frame, instill new ideas/creativity and require follow through by participants.

§ Harness the Power of the Pen - Challenge every employee to refine their written communication skills (e-mail, letters, proposals) to incorporate reader perspective, condense word use (and then condense some more) and reread before finalizing. Functional manager should cite examples of well-tuned documents to review at department meetings.

§ The Law of Negativity - One unhappy employee detracts exponentially from co-worker productivity; inaction and complacency translates to an acceptance of these de-motivational behaviors. Communicate with, coach and as a last step terminate your "negative influences".

§ Applaud Different Levels of Job Competency - Indians, not just Chiefs are required to drive functional performance. Be realistic about the competencies of each employee and their potential upside. The clerical employee who works at 90% productivity and possesses an upbeat attitude is a crucial part of business success, despite their inability or lack of desire to move up the corporate ladder.

4

Ingredients For A "Cool" Company

The definition of "cool" varies based upon gender, life status and experience. Maybe that is just the point, a cool company pieces together a collection of different generations with different expectations to not just blend, but harness the collective energies and knowhow of the components.

§ **Create Energy, Even in a Stagnant Workplace** - Too often, professionals describe their monotonous work environment, where daily business is anything but exciting. In order to change this environment, be nimble, carefree and risk tolerant (especially when so many are risk averse). Some of the best ways workplace energy is produced:

Sales and Revenues create Energy.
Client Care creates Energy.
Creative Ideas create Energy.
Laughter creates Energy.
Relationships create Energy.
Women create Energy.
Teams and Teamwork create Energy.
Receptionists (no kidding!) create Energy.
True leaders create Energy.
But most of all, YOU create Energy.

What's does the energy-meter say about you and your co-workers today?

§ The Fallacy of Open Door Policies - Business executives often pride themselves on an "open door policy". The reality is that many employees will not broach issues and ideas unless they are invited through this open door. Your success is the result of keen instincts and problem resolution; don't leave the first step of necessary communication to subordinates.

§ Holiday Cheer- Stand Out, Be Different - December is chaotic, predictable and tiring, both on a business and a personal level. To mix things up, send holiday cards and gifts in November and have a Holiday Party in January to kick-off the New Year, rather than add to the already crowded (and often, stressful) Yuletide social schedule.

§ Any of These "Wish List Items" Ring True? -

- Improve consistency, "tone" and delivery of workplace communication... to decrease sensitivity and instill employee empowerment, confidence and passion.
- Embrace direct and formalized interaction vs. email.
- Enhance management information and analysis to zero in on important trends, stimulate organizational responsiveness and increase profitability.
- Ask and then require all internal functions to "raise the performance bar"
- Focus on scalable growth... stressing differentiation, end user "benefits", and long-term relationship orientation.
- Market to your customer needs; sell intelligently, persistently and professionally.
- Create a pleasant, cohesive work environment... to augment recruiting initiatives, spur employee motivation and business productivity.
- Challenge key managers to be exemplary leaders.

§ Rethink Your Mission Statement - Look at your Mission Statement. Are the words "revenue, customer and "talent" (or some derivation thereof) present? If not, take pen to paper and create a more impacting statement to incorporate these three universal "keys" to business prominence.

§ Innovation is Where It's At - Unless you are lucky enough to own a patent, your brand better be fresh and engineered for today. Feed your core business cogs, customers and employees with lots of healthy innovation and excitement… continuously.

§ The "Skinny" Regarding Compensation – Compensation paid at below market rates (although today, what constitutes market is highly debatable) does not always equate to unhappy, unproductive employees. A motivating, consistent workplace combined with career growth opportunities and being part of something exciting can be adequate replacements for a few thousand dollars in a more combative environment. Little "perks" and a supportive nurturing atmosphere go a long way for mainstream employees to feel good about their job.

§ Do You Really Need an Industry Specific Consultant? - Conformity to industry norms will not differentiate your company or motivate your employees to build on organizational strengths and competitive advantages. Take pride in your unique business model and internal personality to harness your true organizational potential rather than sticking to what same old, same old preaches.

§ Friend and Consulting Mix Like Oil and Water -
Utilizing personal relationships in business is a dangerous game. Your key hires were brought in through arms-length processes; settling for trust over competency results in mediocrity and often an arduous, stressful path to separation.

§ Amplify your Customers and Employees Pulse -
The economy continues to be weak, meaning your customers are more conservative, your competitors more aggressive (or desperate) and your employees more combustible. Attack these challenges head on by taking a snapshot of employee and/or customer attitudes to protect what you have and strengthen your brand, staying ahead of the curve... and the economy.

§ Focus on the Delivery, Not the Deliverable -
Deliverables is an overused piece of business jargon. While output is of tremendous importance; equally important is the cohesion, teamwork, and processes to get there, and the necessary change required as dictated by the global strategy.

§ Eliminate Us vs. Them Mentality - Sales, operations, finance, IT and administration are all part of the same organization and the same team. Implement work-related and team building type programs where all employees feel good about the Company and interrelate better with their fellow employees, no matter what their function.

§ Facilitate Open Communication - The grapevine or rumor mill at many Companies is a tremendous pipeline of information. A realistic balance of power between core organizational functions (sales, operations and finance) and enhanced communication throughout all functions ensures effective siphoning of information. In a more closed environment, this information is often debilitating.

§ Reduce the Intimidation Factor - Intimidation tactics may be used in certain communications with external relationships (still of questionable value), but have extremely limited benefit with employees. You want employees to be motivated by growth, profits and shared success, not fear.

§ The "First Human Impression" in Your Company - The core job requirements of a front desk person are personality, personality and personality. Whether greeting incoming phone calls, in-person customers, or dealing with problems, the front desk person represents a critical voice and perception of your organization. If you have a front desk person that is friendly, outgoing and consistent in their interpersonal care, you have a winner.

§ Status Quo is Never OK - Communicate to all employees expectations of continuous improvement internally (within the organization) and externally (to impact the customer experience). Every employee must maintain organized lists of recommendations for improvement and communicate these with frequency for the purposes of meetings, constructing goals and driving organizational success.

§ "Guiding Principles" for Your Organization -
Focus on 6-8 key positive acronyms to "buy into" with memorable descriptions describing the essence of your Company focus, strategy and differentiators. Stress the positive atmosphere and confidence which your employees feel proud to live by in their common business world. These Guiding Principles are also highly useful "sales tools" for both recruiting and selling purposes (and as part of a "leave behind" in either situation).

5

The Elite Rungs Of Leadership Success

Yes, great leaders are born. But even the best leaders can't perform unless they are aligned with the right knowledge and the right people at the right time. Leadership traits, instincts and actions must be honed, strengthened and developed over time similar to the muscles in our body or the exquisite taste of a fine wine.

§ **Minimize Interruptions to Maximize Focus and Energy** – While great for leaders to be approachable, this trait must actually be monitored to drive key employees forward. Employees should not bring up issues unless they have developed a suggested solution and have reviewed it with their manager. Even direct reports must refine their communication with leaders (except for very important, immediate resolution items) to weekly dialogue. At middle management levels, the manager must be more readily available for day to day needs, but the dialogue must still be productive, not interruptive.

§ **Leader Interactions Impacts Employee Actions** – Leaders ability to influence and impact others (both internally and externally) is immeasurable- when delivered effectively, you escalate organizational engagement and alignment, when delivered the wrong way it is stifling and heightens de-motivation, sensitivity and performance.

§ Don't Compare Yourself to Others - Leaders walk a different walk, live a different life, breathe a different air. As a leader you must be compassionate, endearing, and supportive to your employees, while constantly pushing for betterment and change. Never communicate frustration to employees regarding your own monetary status- i.e. "I have not received a raise in several years." No one worries, cares about or necessarily believes your challenges.

§ Attack Collaboration Challenges "Head On" - Executives must learn to like (at a minimum respect/tolerate) each other on both a personal level and a business level. They must first examine themselves and commit to improve their own actions, communications and congeniality. They must truly work as part of a team, rather than a jigsaw puzzle that does not fit together. Commit to lunch to share ideas and get to know each other better. Conduct executive management meetings once a month out of the office for lunch or dinner. Bring in an outside facilitator to improve communication and attack problems. Understand that you won't always agree with your peer's decision, but you will respect them, learn from them, and communicate in a professional and understanding manner. The result will be reduction in the number of closed door meetings, and improved motivation and cohesion throughout.

§ Reduce "Impromptu" Closed Door Meetings - Time spent in "hush hush" discussions among the executives in smaller organizations should be evaluated and often reduced. Executive managers have to constantly remember their primary goals and responsibilities, lead, manage, develop, plan and execute, most of which is best navigated by "presence", not "absence".

§ "Touch" Employees Consistently – Your employees require interaction and status updates from your leaders. Leadership communications are magnified five-ten times due to perceived power in the eyes of mainstream employees. Consider "town hall meetings" to feed employees desire for information and face time. These meetings can alternate functions and locations and will include plenty of praise, honest communication about future challenges and opportunities, and answers to questions submitted in advance and at the meeting (don't expect too many of these). Be confident employees are highly appreciative of this format even if they don't communicate to that effect.

§ Need More Chiefs rather than Indians – Careful of functions (or even entire organizations) where everyone is working in the detail and acting more like an Indian (even the so-called business leaders). In these circumstances, management oversight is virtually non-existent, innovation and creativity is squashed (due to lack of motivation and "fire") and execution of key tasks is done at a 60% commitment level with 60% effort- not 110% commitment level with 110% effort. The managerial and director level employees need to "step up" in order to lead, delegate and support organizational & strategic initiatives.

§ A Very Precious Asset – Too much time is lost due to "fires" that should be extinguished by your direct reports. Empower talented managers and require unparalleled attention, responsiveness and results in their areas of accountability.

§ Candor is a Good, Up to a Point - Open communication is a key ingredient to drive organizational success, but don't go too far. Different individuals will interpret, internalize and take advantage of the same set of information in different ways; the more sensitive and delicate the "data", the risk of combustion increases. Time required to extinguish fire and repercussions from misinterpreted information is often not equitable to the initial "perception of benefit".

§ Empower Employees thru Confidence Building - Have confidence that key personnel are capable of making key day to day decisions without your intimate involvement and in turn, help them to understand what to inform you about and what they can handle without your approval. You must be able to "push down" communications with your managers to only relevant information truly requiring your attention as it relates to human capital and business tactics.

§ Chess Anyone? - Building a sound organizational structure can be likened to a chess game. Instead of plotting pawns and rooks, you plot people and positions. Just like chess, every piece on your playing board, every strategic move impacts future results. Ensure your organizational pieces are properly assessed, aligned and revamped based upon changing needs and tactics, from knights to customer relations, bishops to department heads.

§ Leaders are Insatiable - Great business leaders are gratified, but never satisfied with their ongoing business accomplishments.

§ Identify the Structure, Then Build It - Detail your ideal organizational structure for the next 3 years and beyond, communicate clearly and hold accountable those core employees responsible for making it happen from a hiring, transition and integration perspective, starting today. Time is always of the essence.

§ Be "Obsessive" in Self-Reflection - Executive management must be dedicated to constant self-reflection, self-examination and strategy adjustment. Such proactive paranoia is rare. In fact, most leaders don't have a clear Plan A they occasionally update, let alone a Plan B. The process of facing reality readily comes only to the most gifted of business visionaries.

§ Nothing Like Undivided Attention - The most impressive leaders are exclusively focused on the conversation at hand- available, responsive and genuine. Are you and other organizational leaders 100% engaged with the individual(s) involved in your telephone or in-person dialogue?

§ Accentuate your Collective Talent - People represent either your obstacle or your path to sustained business success. Recognize competent employees and be accepting of their minor human flaws. Terminate employees who lack value or create ongoing disruption. Key employees must be gifted, assume full accountability in their responsible function(s) and be well respected amongst their peers.

§ Who is your Sounding Board? - Successful executives utilize a sounding board to expand creativity, fortify strategic vision and solidify decision making. Whether the objective listener is your spouse, friend or colleague, the individual should possess an adept understanding of people and well-rounded business acumen.

§ Be Approachable - Respect between employees and management is often a factor of "approachability". Executives need to welcome questions, ideas and problems, and commit time to the solutions and provision of feedback in a positive, constructive manner.

§ Gimme a Break! - In the age of Blackberries, cell phones and information overflow, the need to re-energize becomes more vital than ever before. When you are on vacation, don't fool yourself by thinking you need to be "in touch". Let's others handle your to do's and you'll come back feeling satiated, refreshed and raring to go.

§ Consistency - A Must Have Trait - We admire Derek Jeter and Warren Buffet for their remarkable consistency in behavior and performance. In the business battlefield, consistency garners managerial respect, stamps future leaders and provides the extra edge for winning business deals and strategy. How consistent are you and your key managers?

§ Spread a Bit of Compassion - Compassion is a vital executive trait. No matter how talented, customer oriented and persistent your best employees are, humans are motivated by a feeling of importance and recognition for their efforts.

§ Leaders focus Strategic 1st, Tactical 2nd - Gifted leaders invest in organizational dynamics in advance of problems and growth challenges, not in reaction to them. The result of this proactive investment is a cohesive workforce, optimization of functional performance and sustained increases in shareholder value.

§ Where Did My Day Go? - Key managers become frustrated when planned tasks are not completed; kicked aside by daily fires and a new set of priorities at day's end. Successful executives and Companies differentiate themselves from these ongoing challenges. They set both short term priorities (daily or weekly) and longer term goals (quarterly) that clarify thinking, actions and execution based upon well thought out game-plans and reassess with frequency.

§ Common TRAPS on the Road to Sustained Leadership Success:

- **Optimize Manager Competencies - My Trusted Employee Isn't That Good TRAP** - Beware of long-term employees/managers whose best contributions to you and your organization are in the past. Skill sets required in 2007 are vastly different than the strategic, proactive focus required for 2011 and beyond.

- **Optimize Revenues - My Focus on a Few Good Customers TRAP** - Successful Companies often have their "bubble burst" by the loss of a customer who represents a significant % of revenues. No matter how strong relationships are, never stop investing in marketing/sales initiatives or product innovation to drive your mid-term and long-term revenue pipelines.

- **Optimize Objectivity- The Family and Friend TRAP** - Repercussions of incorporating personal relationships into your business increase stress for you and increase friction within your organization. Managed growth requires an objective focus regarding your personnel's ability to contribute; not one complicated by non-business related matters.

- **Optimize Number Crunching Prowess - My Accounting Department is Overhead TRAP** - Interpreted… you don't have a Controller or CFO who understands (or has been mentored to understand) the big picture and provides insight, information and controls required to support executive management, sales and operations. If your instincts tell you accounting & finance is "dragging you down", don't push these feeling aside… take action.

§ Traits Indicative of Emerging Leaders –

- **Stress Common Goals** - Define, redefine and publish organizational & departmental goals, revenues and measures of success.

- **Communicate Honestly and Openly** – Ask their people what they like and don't like about the workplace. Provide consistent positive and constructive feedback.

- **Demand Mutual Respect and Hard Work** - Create an environment where employees feel pride in their own accomplishments.. and those of co-workers.

- **Share Knowledge and Experience** – Achieve employee job satisfaction through effective recruiting, hands-on training and mentoring to create and accelerate the performance of future stars.

6

Formulate A Great Company

No matter the industry or size, all Companies strive for continual improvement. Without the statistical machinations, let's agree that all of us need to step back from our sea of priorities and simply ask, How Can We Improve?

§ Identify and Achieve Your Organizational Goals:

Company Goals
- Increase shareholder value.
- Derive positive cash flow.
- Provide an environment where employees learn, grow and have fun.
- Provide a commitment to customer service second to none; embraced by each employee, valued by every customer.

Obstacles You Must Overcome to Achieve Company Goals
1. Lack of understanding regarding customer and employee needs.
2. Sales function that does not embrace the persistent, professional approach required to land key customers.
3. Short-term revenue gain at the expense of long-term profitability.

Departmental Goals
- Sales creates customer opportunities and solutions.
- Operations creates and implements customer solutions.
- Accounting establishes internal controls, manages cash flow and produces data for informed decision making.
- Human Resources ensures that external growth and internal competencies are in sync.

Obstacles You Must Overcome to Achieve Department Goals
1. Lack of balance and cohesion among departments.
2. High performing sales and marketing functions in combination with mediocre accounting and/or human resources functions.

Structural Goals
- Staff personnel follow directions and execute tasks effectively.
- Middle management is effective at idea creation, implementation, organization and staff development.
- Executive management strategize, plan, empower and communicate consistently and at a high level.

Obstacles You Must Overcome to Achieve Structural Goals
1. Lack of effective personnel and structure with "cracks" most often found in middle management functions.
2. Reactive rather than proactive response to business challenges.
3. Inadequate communication from both direct supervisors and Company visionaries.

§ Know Where the Grass Grows - Employees worth keeping in your organization demand growth, a cohesive management team and effective communication. If you are

not delivering in these critical "value" areas, expect problems to arise, engagement to suffer and turnover to increase.

§ Change "Organizational Mindset" from Reactive to Proactive -

Proactivity occurs through embracing accountability, job clarity and a goal oriented focus that extends beyond today and this week. Communicate, reward and collaborate with frequency; ensure all key employees understand their role and responsibilities in upgrading a burgeoning organization to a top quality Company.

§ Plan for and Visualize Success - As you embark upon

each new quarter and year, business focus turns to market share, implementation, execution and growth. Ask yourself and answer honestly: Is your leadership team equipped with the knowledge, tools and goals to carry out your Company's vision?

§ Benefits of a "Sound" Organizational Structure -

An effective structure reduces issues stemming from lack of "trust" as a motivated, cohesive executive team embraces their roles, communicates them effectively and demands results from their responsible employee teams.

§ Establish Clean Lines of Reporting - Job functions

where an employee reports to more than one manager, or where the reporting responsibilities are not clear creates confusion. Tough to hold managers accountable for an employee's actions or development where they do not have full control.

§ Be the Meat, Not the Fat - Too often, Companies are staffed for the past, rather than the future. Don't be the fatty spare rib where you get a succulent taste, but you won't be buying them again at that restaurant. Assess and reassess the "meatiness" of your organization from implementation to communication, accountability to managerial knowhow.

§ Identify the Customer – Many internal functions lack clarity as to who their customer is. Information technology and accounting/finance must recognize their core customers as other departmental functions. The ability to serve customer needs at the highest level is a critical determinant of functional (and organizational) success.

§ What are Employees and Customers Thinking? - Gather employee perspectives and analyze this feedback to enhance organizational structure, effectiveness and communication. Consider utilizing an objective outsider with these initiatives to heighten the likelihood of meaningful, candid insights.

§ Question Your Manager's Management Skills - Employing managers who can't manage stunts your growth. Determine if skill enhancement can be achieved with minor investments of time and dollars or if should just cut your losses through reassignment or paths toward termination.

§ Business is Business – Needs change over time. Long-term employees who were once key cogs may no longer be able to produce in a newer, more vibrant organization. Business leaders cannot err in putting allegiance over productivity.

§ Preach Accountability and Develop Goals – Every business function must identify recurring and non-recurring goals to be completed in a succinct time period (ideally quarterly). These goals can begin the formulation of a Company-wide goal implementation plan, and will ensure enhancements are not just desired, they are required. In order for goals to be effective they need to be measurable- a sales goal of developing quality new relationships is not measurable, whereas the goal of making at least 25 calls in a day is measurable. Each manager should be responsible for developing quarterly goals with their staff that are simplistic and challenging.

§ You Have to Feel Uncomfortable to Drive Sustained Business Momentum –

- Accepting mediocrity in employee performance, attitude or responsiveness leads to loss of internal motivation and external customer goodwill.
- The most important trait an executive can possess is "passion". The most important trait a manager possesses is "accountability".
- In the eyes of employees, you can never expend enough time on communicating. In the eyes of your marketplace and market share, you can never expend enough effort on marketing.

§ What Value Am I Getting from External Advisors? - Retaining your outside accounting firm and other external relationships (financial service advisor, attorney) based upon convenience and trust, rather than performance borders on ludicrous, but it happens more often than not.

§ Implement Regularly Scheduled Meetings - Like them or not, meetings are crucial to business success. They are used to develop teamwork, brainstorm, solve problems, disseminate information, ensure consistent and accurate communication, "touch" and motivate employees, and ensure various functions are operating effectively and collaboratively. Use stories (good and bad) to illustrate points on success, obstacles and lessons learned. These meeting types and frequency are essential:

- *Company Meeting- Monthly or Quarterly* (Approximately 90 minutes) – Run by the CEO (or business unit president) with remote employees "piped in". Ask for questions in advance, publish an agenda, stick to the timeframe and maintain list of all ideas and follow ups required.

- *Sales Meeting- Semi Monthly or Monthly* (Approximately 90 minutes) - Run by the VP sales incorporating sales personnel only (except in circumstances where an outside perspective is beneficial- i.e. motivation from outside the organization or procedural from inside the organization). Siphon information from metrics to discuss revenues, trends, pipeline information, number of calls, leads generated etc. Consider publishing results by salesperson if "competition" will drive sales productivity.

- *Functional Meetings- Semi Monthly or Monthly* (i.e. IT, operations, accounting) - Each functional leader to hold monthly meetings with their staff to address ongoing opportunities or obstacles in the Company or within their function. Key insights from these meetings should be brought to executives' attention.

- *Special Project Meetings* – Discussion of key projects, problems and opportunities- timeframe and participants as required.

Most meetings require the following details in order to be effective:

1. **Agenda** - (with requests for items delivered one/two days prior)
2. **Concise Time Frame** – with agenda items discussed.
3. **Leader/Facilitator** - must be a charismatic manager empowered to guide and make decisions. Consider co-heads for meetings which are cross –functional.
4. **Task Identification and Minutes** – Distributed within a succinct timeframe thereafter.

§ Assess thru Consistent, Hands-On Employee Oversight - Top managers and leaders learn the capabilities of every responsible employee (including themselves), and understand how they perform in slow times, busy times and stressful times. Executive management must devise the plan, ready the troops, press the buttons, and assume total accountability for challenges to be met and exceeded. Unilateral thinking is never acceptable; success requires continual camaraderie, communication and alignment.

§ Make Every Day Month End – Companies often have a month end push, creating tremendous stress on production, accounting and sales. This stop and start mentality accepts a modest pace stepped up to hectic in the last week of the month to make numbers and catch up. Progress, hard work and sound implementation are every day goals, whether the calendar reads Friday the 13th, the 1st Tuesday in April or the 30th of September.

§ 10 Core Questions to Stimulate Success -

1. Passion…Are you as motivated and confident today as you have ever been?
2. Vision… Have you identified your mid-term (this quarter, one year) and long-term business goals (3-5 years)?
3. Competency…Are your employees talented enough to get you there?
4. Structure…Is your management team committed, accountable and responsive?
5. Dynamics…Are your employees motivated and working cohesively?
6. Teamwork…Do your departmental functions respect one another and work effectively together?
7. Management Information…Is your internal financial house running optimally?
8. Hunters…Are your salespeople focused, professional and hungry?
9. Referrals…Are your customers/clients satisfied with your value proposition?
10. Name Recognition…Do your "class A" prospects know who you are? Do you know who they are?

§ Differentiation is of Immense Importance– Think differentiation regarding tactical and strategic priorities:

- *Differentiate your Marketing Approach* - through high quality, "crisp" communication and presentation materials. Ensure consistent "image", branding and name recognition as the foremost goals of your e-mail and letter writing campaigns, marketing handouts and website.

- *Differentiate your Sales Goals* - by stressing performance and measurement tools in advancing relationships, not just closing deals. Mandate all salespeople to spend a minimum of 25% effort in cold calling or more affectionately, "hunting" initiatives.

- *Differentiate your Customer Perspectives* - by accepting only the highest levels of quality and responsiveness from every employee. Seek customer feedback to understand the "differentiators" of doing business with you vs. the competition. Ensure customer service maintain personalization and satisfaction in the hand-off from sales to operations/production/distribution/project management.

- *Differentiate your Accounting Function* - by requiring timely, accurate, concise management information to impact executive decision making. Ensure finance team leaders and staff work cohesively with other departmental functions.

- *Set Goals for all Department Managers to Differentiate Themselves* - by successfully balancing the accountability for departmental excellence with the ongoing necessities of staff development, training and communication.

- *Differentiate your Internal Communication* - with credibility, mutual respect and consistency. Recognize the immense power of your words –both negative and positive. Clarify your strategic focus and align your organizational structure, your advisors and your capital with the means to get there.

• *Differentiate Personal Relationships* - with employees and advisors to remain objective regarding the required skill sets and personalities necessary to successfully execute and grow.

§ Why Doesn't Every Business. . .

• *Keep People Happy?* - Because we are all human. Keep managers focused on consistent problems, not petty issues which are typically short-lived. Recognize you will grow beyond certain employee skill sets.

• *Say No!* - To the manager who can't manage, the salesperson not carrying their weight, to the customer eroding margins.

• *Count to 10?* - Numbers don't lie. A rock solid accounting & finance function tells you where you've been, where you're going and is essential to sustained profitability. Don't settle for average in this incredible important area. Evaluate and if necessary, ramp up your financial know-how and competencies now.

• *Invest in the Hiring Process?* – Bad hires are inevitable, but delayed reaction time to mediocre employees is unacceptable. Objectively evaluate your infrastructure for "gaps", hire slow, fire fast and ensure hiring decision makers understand what's necessary to assess and attract real talent.

§ Value Comes in Many Shapes and Sizes - As MasterCard has successfully branded, real and intangible value doesn't always equal a $ figure. Consider crucial facets of your organization, i.e. recruiting, sales management, internal accounting, structure, accountability; all carry a heavy weight towards meeting and exceeding your strategic goals. You might call upgrades in these areas... "Priceless".

§ My Outside Accounting Firm Handles That - Accounting Firms have utilized their "trusted advisor" role to branch off into consulting, recruiting and financial services. Be wary of letting your number crunching experts versed in tax and technical accounting also be your organizational and personal financial experts. The price can be high and "real world" internal business expertise is often lacking.

7

Sales And Marketing For All Seasons

Effective marketing and branding strategies in conjunction with driven business development talent is tantamount to job creation and sustained organizational prowess. Nevertheless, sales and marketing is often envied because they get bigger budgets and work less. Ensure your key employees recognize and embrace the value of sales and marketing.

§ Seek Qualitative Feedback from Customers & Prospects – Use an objective outsider to poll current, past and future customers to gauge their likes and concerns about working with your organization. Engage a firm and/or individuals who grasp phone communication and data accumulation with no axes to grind or allies to protect.

§ Open New Doors Continuously - If your business requires hunters, and your salespeople don't "get it" or don't "do it", you lose money, time and goodwill. The art of cold calling when done right is more impacting than ever before... identify those who "get it" and embrace them to open new doors and drive revenues.

§ **Sales to Assist the Collections Process** – Sales personnel must communicate A/R terms upfront to their customer contacts and share that internal accounting and collections function can be a real bear if these terms are not maintained.

§ **If You Are Type 'A', Come to Papa** – Segregating customers by sales potential between "type A, B and C" (attention paid, follow up, etc) is essential. Accelerate the relationship with top tier - type A customers and identify, market and sell to prospective customers with this same potential. Divvy out relationships to those who can most effectively handle and drive revenues with these layers.

§ **Sales Assessment Requires Direct Observation** – No matter how effective sales training, metrics and management are, assessing and enhancing sales skills is predicated on observing their performance in front of the customer. Management and coaching are only partially effective when dealing with "perceptions" rather than a more hands-on approach.

§ **Embrace Voice Mails** – Some counsel sales professionals to not leave "voice mails"; an antiquated and totally inefficient tactic. Effective cold calling requires persistency, name recognition and some level of trust/comfort before getting the meeting. Voice mail messages allow the prospect to assess interest level on their own terms, also allowing the caller to perfect their communication, delivery and salesmanship (or sales-person-ship).

§ Relationships 1st, Business Next - Closed deals (and repeat business) are frequently the result of information gathering, sustained effort, trust and relationship development in advance of the time the purchase decision is made. Business development professionals must excel in all facets of the sales cycle, not just the sale.

§ Good Things Came to Sales Professionals Who Persist - Too often, salespeople (and companies) fail to recognize the value of mid-term (3 months- 1 year) and longer-term prospective customers (1 year +) due to the priorities of the minute and the pressure to close, close, close. Leadership must consistently preach the benefits of relationship development and follow up. As a salesman builds his or her "book" the mid-term opportunities from 3 months ago and the long-term opportunities from last year develop a consistent flow contributing to increased revenues and... commissions.

§ Embrace the Telephone as "The" Sales Tool - The telephone is a great tool to drive relationships, reinforce name recognition, personalize the sale and close deals. Challenge every business development professional (and hold them accountable) to make 100 calls per week and watch revenues escalate rapidly. Don't be frustrated by the lack of a call back, every quality salesperson knows the telephone is a processing game, each voice mail is an opportunity to put a "feeler" in a prospective customers mind. Three, five or ten phone calls are often necessary to make contact, establish rapport and move the relationship from Point A to Point B.

§ **Marketing & Name Recognition** - An extremely successful client provided the following food for thought: "When planning the marketing and advertising budget for the following year- detail the anticipated expenditures and double them. There is no greater stimulus to long-term success than a solid marketing plan and a focused commitment behind it".

§ **Grab the Decision Maker's Attention, the Old Fashioned Way** - Utilize "Snail Mail" to achieve name recognition, to express genuine gratitude following the advancement of a relationship, to gradually introduce the benefits of your product or service. Letter writing and direct marketing stand out in a sea of stimuli, reflecting personalization, effort and impact not achievable through phone or e-mail communication.

§ **Knock, Knock; Anybody Home?** – Decision makers are often strangely elusive rather than forthcoming after a quality meeting, deciding to ignore multiple calls and emails. Although "yes", "no" or "timing not right" is more efficient feedback, the lack thereof may not be reflective of your approach, but their own insecurities or poor communication in chaotic times. Try different angles to move up their priority list, but always be careful to respect their precious time.

§ **Networking is Not a Substitute for Business Development** - Sales efforts focused on direct lines to the decision maker is typically preferable to spending time with "pathways" to that decision maker. While networking is a strong complement to core selling strategy, be wary of the loss of control and inefficiency towards end revenue production.

§ Use "The Age of Massive Media" to Your Advantage

- Media today is omnipresent with 500 TV channels, publications littering every industry and the burgeoning potential of social networking. Utilize Public Relations to harness these massive marketing opportunities and accelerate name recognition, brand loyalty and revenues. But make sure to hold your PR firm or internal personnel assigned these tasks accountable for results.

§ Is Cold Calling Dead or is Your Salesperson's Attitude?

- A flurry of business people have told us; "no one cold calls anymore". Unfortunately for them, mediocrity either in themselves or their salespeople is being accepted. Bottom line, cold calling in a persistent and professional manner is a vital tool to get in front of important decision makers. Admittedly, it doesn't work for the "faint of heart".

§ Listen to Unspoken Signals from the Sales Prospect

- Prospects may request information and never respond to the salesperson's two or three follow up phone calls. Rather than labeling these customers as "not interested", consider their initial interest as a sign that they will purchase your product or service, but the timing is not right. Follow up contacts including direct mailing, quarterly phone calls and e-mails will keep the relationship development angle going and increase the likelihood that when ready to buy, they will realize the value of partnering with you and your brand.

§ **Turn Potential into Performance** - Will the "forever discussed" pipeline your team members promise result in closed deals? To differentiate embellishment from reality, utilize tools/metrics to monitor performance, facilitate semi-monthly meetings to evaluate revenue expectations and hold sales personnel accountable for exceeding production goals.

§ **Embrace the Power of Public Speaking** - A long-time client speaks proudly of his company's evolution 40 years ago. His father literally created the market for their unique, highly technical manufacturing process through presentations given to targeted industry and user groups. Public speaking represents a highly cost effective marketing tool to achieve name recognition, trust, and to open the door to new relationships and revenue opportunities.

§ **Tap into your Customer Demands** – Quality sales professionals must consistently ask for and listen to customer & sales channel insight. This knowledge must be diced, sliced and brainstormed for enhanced product focus, pricing strategies and strategic maneuvering throughout the organization.

§ **Embrace Door Opening Opportunities** – There is "untapped" opportunity to attract customers the old-fashioned way, combining letter writing, in-person visits (if geographically feasible) and phone solicitations (just a few calls/voice mail messages and these are transitioned to warm calling). The door opener does not have to be the closer, but they must embrace your product/service and be persistent, relationship focused and professional.

§ Managerial Oversight without the Manager – Smaller companies may lack a sales leader to drive change, creativity and revenue growth. The role is often "assumed" by a top producer, stretched thin with multiple priorities or lacking strategic knowhow. As alternatives, consider external sales training to deliver fresh ideas and renewed energy or hire a customer relations manager to support customer needs while improving processes, productivity, controls and effectiveness throughout the selling cycle.

§ Nothing Better than The Sales High - Salespeople love the thrill of accelerating a prospect forward, affectionately coined the "sales high".

§ Persistency Always Prevails! - Opening new sales "doors" is a complex equation of clarifying benefits, understanding needs and assessing timeframe ... in combination with dedication, passion and persistence. Barriers of entry to high level decision makers are perforated only by business development professionals willing to go the extra mile, recognizing their messages (voice mails, emails, letters), while often unreturned, are not unnoticed.

§ Seek Salespeople with "Hunter Mentality - Companies are requiring a "hunter mentality" when recruiting sales professionals, another business catch phrase representing a new way of looking at old principles. Impacting sales professionals are hungry, persistent, professional, knowledgeable and confident. Hunters are adept at cold calling (via telephone and in-person), and develop relationships and close sales based upon a cultivated understanding of the customers' needs.

8

You Can't Fake Math

There are some areas of business that you have to understand. Interpersonal communication and management skills are obvious, but equally important and perhaps a bit more "in the shadows" is the need to understand accounting & finance. Numbers are crucial to evaluate historical results, identify trends/opportunities, fine-tune decision making and evaluate the validity of new ideas. While no one expects Albert Einstein, you have to push yourself to be cognizant of numbers to fine-tune your knowledge and performance.

§ **Make Financial Information Meaningful** – Financial statements often lack excitability for the end-user. Quality internal business information is succinct, comparative and heightens reader knowledge and decision making capabilities. Specifics include:

- Comment on all trends worthy of executive attention.
- Compare operating results to both prior periods and budgets with variances and explanations of positive/negative trends. Prior periods should reflect the three prior months for monthly financials (and comparable time period from prior year) and the three prior quarters for quarter end financials.
- Provide detail within summary expense classifications- 4 or 5 key categories within selling expense, general and administrative expenses. Examples include salaries, commission, insurance expense, rent expense, telephone expense, office expense, etc.

- Ask key executives what analysis and metrics are useful for them to make key decisions regarding their area of accountability and collaborate to fulfill their requests.
- Controllers and key financial personnel should spend time with key managers to enhance their understanding of financial statements and related information. This serves a dual purpose of enhancing critical knowledge and accelerating relationships.

§ **Understand and Talk the "Budget Game"** - Ensure you truly understand the budget process from beginning to end as this is escalating in importance from both a planning and adherence perspective. Ask trusted colleagues either internally or outside of your organization to drill the concepts into your head at an intellectual, rather than just a service level.

§ **Conduct Timely Discussion to Review Financial Information** - Disseminate financial results in a formal meeting (quarterly) with key decision makers to address questions and ensure focus on crucial trends.

§ **Give the "Perception" of Inventory Control** - Only key employees involved in inventory control processes need to know if there is not an extensive inventory tracking mechanism in place. In organizations where inventory is a cost of doing business rather than the reason for doing business (i.e. software) the extensive cost of controlling inventory may not deliver an effective cost-benefit return. Perception is half the battle in controlling shrinkage and implementing effective safeguards over assets.

§ When Analyzing Trends, Count to 3 - Compare key performance indicators over the prior three months, three quarters and three years. For example, analyzing revenues (and margins) by customer, salesperson and product mix over these timeframes will improve knowledge of business performance and provide the insight to heighten sound decision making.

§ Utilize an Outside Payroll Processing Firm - There are few no-brainers in life, but one is to utilize an outside payroll processing company rather than handling it internally (except in larger, multi-location companies). ADP, Paychex, and Ceridian all represent low cost, efficient ways to process payroll and relieve the administrative burden of paperwork and tax filings. For whatever reason (fees?) small accounting firms continue to process payroll (and their small company clients let them). PEO are also viable solutions to further ease the administrative hassle of both payroll and benefits, but beware of "hidden costs".

§ Track "Pass Through" Revenues and Costs – In project based businesses, revenues and expenses are incurred, accounted for and passed along to the client through invoicing and billing procedures. To track most effectively, set up "contra" accounts in the general ledger where reimbursable expenses or "pass through" costs are effectively tracked alongside the corresponding billings. Assign an accountant to review these accounts monthly to ensure all reimbursable expenses are being charged and collected from the client- i.e. no money is being left on the table.

§ Collections Opportunities and Enhancements –

Collections efforts are maximized with consistent "touches" of the customer in a professional, but assertive manner. Make friendly collection calls once the balances have hit 45 days (presuming net 30 day terms) and "turn up the heat" as the receivables get older or customer promises are not fulfilled. A simple truth in any accounts payable function (especially during tight cash flow); pay the "pests" who call frequently and vendors you like, ignore the others as long as possible. Recognize also, that sending customer statements are frequently garbage material when received by your customer.

§ Utilize Vendors as a Money Source –

Payroll, employee expense reports and certain recurring monthly bills (phone, rent, etc.) have required payment dates. Other vendor disbursements are ideally paid between 35-45 days after invoice receipt. As long as there is consistency and reasonableness in the timeliness of payments, vendors will be satisfied. In the case of a "cash crunch", a friendly phone call from your accounts payable staff person and you can extend payment for another 15-20 days. Always take advantage of vendor term discounts provided (i.e. 1%, net 10), wherever available, as long as cash flow permits.

§ Step up the Focus on Vendor Relations -

A customer driven organization focuses on responsiveness and follow-through to ensure total customer satisfaction. But who is accountable for vendor relations? Your top 10 vendors account for a sizable % of non-labor related costs; ensure these relationships are sound and are consistently evaluated for quality, service and price. Big companies "get it" and have achieved significant ROI from investment in savvy centralized purchasing functions over the last decade.

9

Your Mental Edge...Fine-Tuned

Life and business are ongoing competitions. We are uniquely in control of our own skills and attitude to ensure that success is continuous, resonating and long-lasting. Invest in yourself and be open to self-reflection and constructive ideas- the rewards will come.

§ Learn From Those You Don't Know - Professionals are often closed minded to new relationships which have the potential to markedly improve business efficiency and reduce stress. Focus on expanding your boundaries beyond the norm to achieve new ideas and attain greater internal gratification. Use your instincts to determine who is worthy of your time and will spark your creative juices, but only after getting past your pre-judgments.

§ Your Words Ring True, Ralph Waldo Emerson - Perhaps you didn't embrace him in high school, but consider the wisdom of Ralph Waldo Emerson, the American poet and philosopher. His quotes and inspiration, easily accessible via mainstream search engines are inspired by the financial crisis of 1837, a confluence of events eerily similar to our recent predicaments. A couple of awe inspiring samples of Ralph Waldo's wisdom:

- "All our progress is unfolding, like a vegetable bud. You have first an instinct, then an opinion, then a knowledge as the plant has root, bud, and fruit. Trust the instinct to the end, though you can render no reason."
- "Character is higher than intellect... A great soul will be strong to live, as well as to think."
- "Every great and commanding moment in the annals of the world is the triumph of some enthusiasm."

§ **The Quiet Truth about Silence** - Effective managers, sales professionals and top recruiting candidates utilize their sound listening skills to exceed their goals and others expectations. Preach effective listening throughout your company to drive creativity, cohesion and customer loyalty.

§ **Dale Carnegie is Genius** – Carnegie's 70 year old timeless classic "How to Win Friends and Influence People" should be required reading for every employee who "touches" the customer or has impact on other employees (and that's every employee). A few of his 30 key concepts with pertinent business applications:

- *"Arouse in the Other Person an Eager Want"* - Do your employees wake up each morning and look forward to the day ahead? Business professionals want recognition, skill set enhancement, quality interactions with co-workers and opportunities for compensation upside (raises, incentives).

- *"Talk in Terms of the Other Person's Interests"* - Sound listening skills and a genuine interest in others, breeds a sense of belonging. If your employees believe managers/executives are on their side; they exude confidence, work harder and deliver results.

- *"Show Respect for Other's Opinion. Never Say You're Wrong"* - Every company suffers "communication breakdowns" resulting from lack of compassion or appreciation for mainstream employees. Tap into your employees unique insights through increased management collaboration and/or external consults to accelerate organizational strengths.

- *"Throw Down a Challenge"* - Whether we've written a New Years resolution or a 2011 quarter 4 revenue target, we are all goal motivated. Set corporate goals which are measurable, functional (by department) and span a realistic time frame (quarterly). But remember, words are just scribbles without actions to back them up.

§ This is a Great Time to be an Employee - Employees have a steady paycheck, benefits and most important, real and tangible opportunity. Now is the time to embrace your situation and truly make a difference.

1. *Forget, for Now, Those Dreams of Your Own Business* - Hey, if you are an entrepreneur with an incredible idea... maybe. But if you want to be a consultant or open a small business, now is not the time! Competition is fierce and the market is lean, demanding and thankless.

2. *Recognize the Pain of Those in Job Transition* - Finding a new job is more stressful and time consuming than you can possibly imagine. Tangible signs of immediate change remain questionable.

3. *Appreciate Your Compensation* – There is tremendous downward pressure on salaries as companies seek to align compensation expense with deteriorating revenues and margins. Your current salary is likely at or above "market value".

4. *Make "You" a Better Manager* - Demand is high for middle managers who balance functional responsibilities in combination with a cognizance for organizational strategies.

5. *Listen and Learn* – Do the extra little things to excel in every business communication. Companies value those who overcome performance barriers and impact customers, vendors and other employees in a highly collaborative manner.

While your job may not be perfect, be very thankful you have one and make every effort to heighten both your attitude and performance. Your level of satisfaction will increase and rewards will come your way. Don't worry about when, right now the reward; "you are employed".

§ Step Back to Step Forward- Every business day, step back for 20 minutes and reflect on your personal business brand, strategies and goals to drive self-improvement.

§ Sign a Truce with Stress and Insecurity -We all experience highs and lows. It is absolutely normal to feel stress or insecurity in areas essential to your business success. Seek people you can confide in and grow from these life challenges, rather than become frustrated and embroiled in a "no-win" battle with "yourself".

§ "House" Ideas and Priorities – The majority of business professionals need to do a better job of "housing their ideas" and following through with their subordinates, their boss and their own priorities. Microsoft Outlook tasks (utilizing categories) or Word tables are excellent tools to ensure today's great ideas are not forgotten tomorrow.

§ Ahhh... The Wonders of Being Alone - I like being by myself. My creative juices flow, my needs are attended to, my movements revolve entirely around me. But the reason why I really appreciate my "alone time" is because I am lucky enough to have a terrific family, good friends and genuinely enjoy people. For that matter, when I'm alone, I spend a fair amount of time pondering over my relationships and my business interactions in an effort to improve them.

If time to myself is too frequent and out of balance with quality social, business and family interactions, the result is counterproductive (i.e. stress, low confidence) instead of maximizing my personal brand for social and business purposes. So I plan for time to myself while I listen, learn and treasure time with others... a very healthy combination indeed!

§ The Power of The "Minds" - Brainstorming is an essential business tool to stir creativity and motivation among employees, management and decision-makers. Effective sessions ensure that worthwhile ideas are followed up for further conceptualization and implementation.

§ Are You Well Connected? - "Well-Connected" is a high compliment in the business world, often equated to likeability, name recognition and trust. Challenge yourself to consistently meet (not just email or talk via the telephone) and develop relationships with those outside of your inner circle: industry performers, decision makers, customers, vendors, savvy business professionals, etc. Your creative juices will be stirred, opportunities will be uncovered, and your personal brand will escalate.

§ Impact your Walk, Talk and Actions with Confidence - Confidence is the "green" in profits, "charisma" in CEO, and "motivate" in manager; an essential human trait to achieve ongoing personal gratification and corporate success. Increase confidence by assessing, challenging and improving the dynamics of your daily life experiences. Don't let your confidence be dragged down due to stress from unresolved personnel challenges, lack of organization, or inability to make difficult decisions

§ The Benefits of Relaxation - An executive who does not take vacation because he/she is too busy or while on vacation is attached to the hip with a Blackberry, is not allowing themselves to re-energize for the challenges ahead. The underlying questions are: What might happen while away and what can be done to instill better controls, structure and staff development to prevent these concerns?

§ Charge" Your Creative Juices thru Peer Coaching - Share challenges and opportunities with respected business associates outside of your organization on a regularly schedule basis (i.e. monthly or quarterly breakfasts). A bit of candor and trust will deliver significant returns in renewed insight, perspective and confidence.

§ Patience & Change Go Hand in Hand - Negative reaction to "change" results from the unknown. For this reason, new managers heightened rules and expectations are always viewed with trepidation at first. Anticipate gradual rather than immediate buy-in during the transition phase. Productive change occurs, quite simply, with the passage of time.

§ **"Passion Counts"** - Companies succeed because their leaders are passionate, and in turn, employees are passionate about what they deliver in the workplace. If you are not giving 100% in focus, drive and commitment, for a hundred different reasons, change ... immediately.

§ **My Neat Little Discovery** - Thanks to my teenage twins, I embrace my i-Pod which clears my head and elevates my focus. Give me sunshine, an hour to sit, walk, run and I'm re-energized; I understand now what the masses before me have discovered.

§ **Expect the Best, Prepare for the Worst** - Everyone is predicting when the business climate will really, truly get better. Be prepared for the worst case scenario as well, what if better is not coming soon?

§ **An Intellectual Bargain** - Business magazines stir your creative juices while relaxing. Annual subscriptions to major business publications (INC, Fortune and Fast Company) are less than $10 in order to pump up reader circulation.

§ **A Gem of a Concept** - A terrific lady emailed me recently saying "I take great pride in working hard every day." If every employee had this approach -we would all be better off and the challenges within management, engagement, collaboration and business success would be so much different.

§ Change Isn't Easy... for Anyone - Recognize business leaders struggle with needed change and enhancements to sustain growth and profitability to an extent greater than their employees.

§ Choose Momentum over Stress - Decision makers often have difficulty overcoming a "soft spot" for a long-tenured, underperforming employee, typically within management. Reduce stress and embrace momentum by overcoming this costly organizational hole.

§ Ideas are Good, Actions are Great - We dwell on our creative ideas and outcomes but struggle to "pull the trigger", especially when change is required. Efficient and effective implementation is predicated on planning, leadership, passion, prioritization and focus, but all is for naught without action.

§ Listen to Your Instincts - Had lunch yesterday with Rob, a long-time business associate. He and I have had tremendous success working together over the years; you might even call it "karma". Funny thing, he gets the credit goes for tremendous persistency in initially developing our relationship, a trait which is usually my forte. Thanks Rob for listening to your internal voice and getting what you wanted; we have both benefited tremendously... Role reversals are oh, so refreshing.

§ Great Advice from Dad - My Dad, 80 years young, gave me great advice a few years ago... "Don't stress about being stressed; it just makes you more stressed."

§ Turn Stale Issues to Fresh Actions -Take control today of the recurring obstacles you face with people, structure, processes, information (or lack of). Trust your instincts, plan the attack and hold yourself (and others) accountable to execute effectively from start to finish.

§ Ask and You Will Receive - Insight gained from effectively worded questions is tantamount to sales, customer service and managerial success. Inquiries should be posed to identify obstacles, improve performance and perception, make better decisions, build relationships and teamwork, and assess capabilities and progress.

§ Thank You Toastmasters - Until 10 years ago, I feared public speaking. But I'm all about positive change for the clients and professionals with whom I work, so I took my own advice and in 2002 joined a local Toastmasters group.

Thirty people from all different walks of life, some very savvy in their presentations, others not. We shared common goals: to support each other, improve our confidence and impact an audience with our unique experiences, spoken word and personal brands. I left Toastmasters in 2005 after achieving the Competent Toastmaster designation (10 speeches) and now present to groups...small and large with only minimal butterflies.

Whether you are an executive, manager or professional in transition, join a local Toastmasters (www.toastmasters.org). Or consider starting Toastmasters in your company as an innovative, fun way to impact relationships, communication and your Company's success. You'll be pleased with your results!

10

Other Thoughts To Ponder

Job Search - In this day and age, any book on business excellence must contain thoughts on this topic. Far too many find ourselves in this mode and the scary truth is the lightening speed in which one week out of a job turns into six months and then one year. Because time is of the essence, the focus, speed and intensity upon which the job seekers acts is essential. Network, network, network in a persistent, but professional manner and don't ever be shy to reach out to professionals who you need to know... and tell them why they need to know you. And never give up, because persistency always prevails!

§ Short Term Thinking Brings Short-Term Benefits
– Professionals often choose their next employer based upon the monetary offer rather than the job, location, company potential and instinct. Focus on the greatest likelihood of maximizing compensation over 5 years, not 6 months.

§ Remember Past Relationships & Affiliations - Seek
alumni networks provided by past employers and universities and on social networking sites. Tap into these affiliations to expand your networking reach and drive your future goals.

§ Words You Shouldn't Hear in an Interview - In my
younger days, I interviewed with an International Real Estate

Holding Company and the process was going terrific with the final step to be a meeting with the high powered, high ego CEO. I sat down in his office, we shook hands, he looked at me straight in the face and the first words out of his mouth were "You don't know !%&$". I lifted my jaw off the floor, looked him straight in the eye and replied, "I disagree" and confidently detailed the ways I would deliver value into his organization. I got the job offer the next day, and said thank you, but no thank you. Lesson learned- intimation motivates no-one, lucky I found out in advance of accepting a job offer.

§ The Paramount Importance of Cover Letters -
Cover letters immediately reveal if the applicant wants this job or just any job. Cover letters tell you who can and who can't write. Inclusion of salary expectations in the cover letter enables decision makers to size up your skills comparatively to your asking price, a great differentiator. The omission of this compensation is akin to shopping for groceries without any price information; you leave the store, immediately.

§ Sustain Momentum After the Elevator Pitch – Sure,
networking functions can be nerve-racking and frustrating. Many develop an effective introduction, but fall short in differentiating their product and service, their knowhow, their personal brand to provide a lasting positive impression. Whether you are on a job interview, selling to an A level prospect or at a networking function, make sure your communication is effective and consistent throughout the process, not just in the beginning stages. Focus on your missteps (often magnified in your own mind) as a means to improve, not a reflection of your entire personal brand.

§ Ask This... Before You Accept the Job Offer - I
helped a friend recently in deciding about an attractive job offer. "Heather" is an operations manager with very

marketable skills and in a long-time situation which has recently soured.

Her offer was attractive, she really liked the two business owners and her instincts said yes. I suggested she respond to the offer with an entrepreneurial company, with one simple request... "I would like to review your financials- I'll sign a confidentiality agreement and the review will be done with you present." The prospective employers' immediate response; "No one has ever asked that before- no way."

Heather is going to work today knowing she made the right decision to stay where she is. And she is much better armed to ensure when she does make a move, it will be the right one.

§ Spice Your Resume and Communications - Promote your prowess w/athletics, music, people and volunteering; skills associated by many with creativity, perseverance and leadership.

For today and the foreseeable future, company decision makers seek initiatives with a predictable cost, defined endpoint, immediate benefits and strong ROI.

§ Frankel Wisdom for the Ages - A great deal of stress within key management and leadership positions is the result of interpersonal challenges. In direct correlation, Talent Management is a "smoking hot" area of business evolvement and will be for the entire 21st century.

§ What are Men Afraid Of? - Resurrecting the Men's Club at my temple a few years back was a tall task. I watched in awe as the Sisterhood grew ever stronger in fund raising, a

sense of community and socialization while the Men's Club struggled despite a thriving congregation.

The reality is men are resistant to stepping outside of their "constants", their inner circle of friends, family and business relationships. Women recognize the value derived from meeting new people and advancing these relationships. Makes me think that the advancement of opportunities for women (and minorities) in business is only in the beginning stages. We'll have hiccups along the way, but great progress is likely.

§ **Ahh...The Benefits of Being Humble** - Donny Deutsch on his former CNBC show, The Big Idea, stated "humble is the new black". Proctor & Gamble has been seeing major opportunity in lower vs. higher priced goods. The seats at major league baseball ballparks are noticeably empty. Two years ago the same radio voice that was selling Lexus is now hawking Mitsubishi. While image is certainly important, we are starting to recognize car leasing, private colleges, big mortgages and Armani clothing may not deliver the returns or the status we originally hoped for.

§ **Be Passionate About Innovation** - So many conversations today are economy focused, representing a cathartic opportunity to understand others' perspectives, overcome our own obstacles and innovate. This historic time period will be remembered as the great equalizer, where the mighty fell, and new leaders and innovators were rewarded. So go ahead, listen, plan, implement, learn from those you don't know and act out of your box!

§ **Twitter- I Guess I Do** - Twitter confuses me. I really, really want to like it. As with "viral marketing", Twitter sounds cool. All the stars are Twittering too. So when I 1st entered the Twitter world, three seconds later, two acquaintances become my Twitter friends. Is their computer immediately "clicked in" to find me or something?

So I get my 5 minute feel for Twitter and I'm just not getting it. Cool people, give me a clue? Any divas around? Please tell me why you care what I am doing moment to moment, thought to thought (except when it affects you) or why I should be caring about what you're doing. Help? Bueller? Please Help!

§ Social Responsibility; Your Time has Come - I've been barraged lately in a quiet manner regarding social responsibility. This is positive and will make our society a better place to live and work.

- Monster.com has beefed up marketing and PR specifically focused on goodwill & social responsibility.
- On LinkedIn, recommendations appeal directly to our sense of social responsibility. A panelist at a major conference I attended reminded us to help struggling friends & colleagues to stay upbeat and well networked.
- The Presenter at a SHRM function (Society for Human Resource Management) I attended last month focused exclusively on the "push down" requirements of corporate social Responsibility to small and mid-sized companies.

What are you doing with your power of social responsibility and ability to pay it forward?

§ Is This The Calm Before The Storm? - Fascinating divergence of perspective between politicians, media types and financial planners who stand to gain the most by believing the recession is waning vs. those most affected by today's economic challenges... business leaders, entrepreneurs and sales professionals who see only minor progress.

I'm witnessing a sense of "calm" from decision makers recently vs. the panic and total lack of clarity prior. No matter what the definition of recession is (didn't the experts not see it as a recession until 6 months after it began?), the majority of us will only feel better once unemployed colleagues and friends are working and small business revenues accelerate; in spite of what the stock market is telling us.

§ Inaction in Business Leads Ultimately to Death –
The colder temperatures don't compare to the "frigidity" and indecisiveness displayed the last few years by many decision makers. Business success is about action, not inaction. Inaction leads to complacency, rumors and decreased everything. Companies who study, create, adjust and ultimately "buy" based upon a well thought out plan of action are the one who will prosper and differentiate themselves.

§ The Day is Coming for Democrats and Republicans to Step Aside – OK, one political/business comment, because I can… In one of the next three elections (10 years), a prominent independent candidate will win the US Presidency (think Ross Perot in more troubling times). We clearly need a break from the politics of politics and there is major work to do in making all areas of government efficient, responsive and financially stable. I marvel at the numbers of business colleagues who agree with me about the solutions- but no politician seems willing to take on the core issues that are not about winning friends, but about good government.

I yearn for a visionary, a really important leader to break the hypocrisy so we can all be confident and proud we that we together as a Country are moving forward in the right, fiscally responsible directions focused on long-term benefit.

Your Notes